AQA (B) GCSE
**Religious Studies**

# Unit 3
# Religion and Morality

**Sheila Butler**

Philip Allan Updates, an imprint of Hodder Education, an Hachette UK company, Market Place, Deddington, Oxfordshire OX15 0SE

*Orders*
Bookpoint Ltd, 130 Milton Park, Abingdon, Oxfordshire OX14 4SB
tel: 01235 827827
fax: 01235 400401
e-mail: education@bookpoint.co.uk
Lines are open 9.00 a.m.–5.00 p.m., Monday to Saturday, with a 24-hour message answering service. You can also order through the Philip Allan Updates website: www.philipallan.co.uk

© Philip Allan Updates 2009
ISBN 978-1-4441-0080-8

First printed 2009
Impression number     6
Year     2014

Illustrations by Jim Watson
Printed in Italy

Hachette UK's policy is to use papers that are natural, renewable and recyclable products and made from wood grown in sustainable forests. The logging and manufacturing processes are expected to conform to the environmental regulations of the country of origin.

P02067

# Contents

# About this book

Revision is vital for success in your GCSE examination. No one can remember what they learned up to 2 years ago without a reminder. To be effective, revision must be planned. This book provides a carefully planned course of revision — here is how to use it.

| *The book* | *The route to success* |
|---|---|
| **Contents list** | **Step 1** Check which topics you need to revise for your examination. Mark them clearly on the contents list and make sure you revise them. |
| **Revision notes** | **Step 2** Each section of the book gives you the facts you need to know for a topic. Read the notes carefully, and list the main points. |
| **Key words** | **Step 3** Key words are highlighted in the text and displayed in key word boxes. Learn them and their meanings. They must be used correctly in the examination. |
| **Test yourself** | **Step 4** A set of brief questions is given at the end of each section. Answer these to test how much you know. If you get one wrong, revise it again. You can try the questions before you start the topic to check what you know. |
| **Examination questions** | **Step 5** Examples of questions are given for you to practise. The more questions you practise, the better you will become at answering them. |
| **Exam tips** | **Step 6** The exam tips offer advice for achieving success. Read them and act on the advice when you answer the question. |
| **Key word index** | **Step 7** On pages 71–72 there is a list of all the key words and the pages on which they appear. Use this index to check whether you know all the key words. This will help you to decide what you need to look at again. |

## *Command words*

All examination questions include **command** or **action** words. These tell you what the examiner wants you to do. Here are the most common ones:

- **Describe** — requires more detail. For example, you may be asked to describe beliefs about life after death in one religion that you have studied.
- **Explain**, **give reasons for** or **account for** — here the examiner is expecting you to show understanding by giving reasons. For example, you may be asked to explain why religious believers hold different views on drinking alcohol.

## Revision rules

- Start early.

- Plan your time by making a timetable.

- Be realistic — don't try to do too much each night.

- Find somewhere quiet to work.

- Revise thoroughly — reading on its own is not enough.

- Summarise your notes, make headings for each topic.

- Ask someone to test you.

- Try to answer some questions from old papers. Your teacher will help you.

**If there is anything you don't understand — ask your teacher.**

## Do you know?

- The exam board setting your paper?

- What level or tier you will be sitting?

- How many papers you will be taking?

- The date, time and place of each paper?

- How long each paper will be?

- What the subject of each paper will be?

- What the paper will look like? Do you write your answer on the paper or in a separate booklet?

- How many questions you should answer?

- Whether there is a choice of questions?

- Whether any part of the paper is compulsory?

**If you don't know the answer to any of these questions as the exam approaches — ask your teacher.**

## Be prepared

### The night before the exam

- Complete your final revision.

- Check the time and place of your examination.

- Get ready your pens, pencil.

- Go to bed early and set the alarm clock.

### On the examination day

- Don't rush.

- Double check the time and place of your exam and your equipment.

- Arrive early.

- Keep calm — breathe deeply.

- Be positive.

## Examination tips

- Keep calm and concentrate.

- Read the paper through before you start to write.

- Decide which questions you are going to answer.

- Make sure you can do all parts of the questions you choose.

- Complete all the questions that you have chosen.

- Don't spend too long on one question at the expense of the others.

- Read each question carefully, then stick to the point and answer questions fully.

- Use all your time.

- Check your answers.

- Do your best.

## Topic 1

# Religious attitudes to matters of life

## Medical research and practice

'Your body is a temple of the Holy Spirit'

Sanctity of life

Life is a gift from God — to be treasured

Life is infinitely precious

## Human genetic engineering

**Genetic engineering** refers to changes made to the genetic structure of living things. Human genetic engineering is permitted for two types of gene therapy: somatic cell therapy and the creation of **saviour siblings**. Some people would like to take genetic engineering further and create **designer babies**.

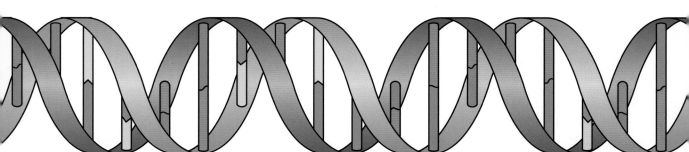

### Somatic cell therapy

This is a treatment that adds to, enhances or replaces a defective gene. It is a treatment for single genetic disorders such as X-SCID (X-linked severe combined immunodeficiency), which means that any infection is likely to prove fatal.

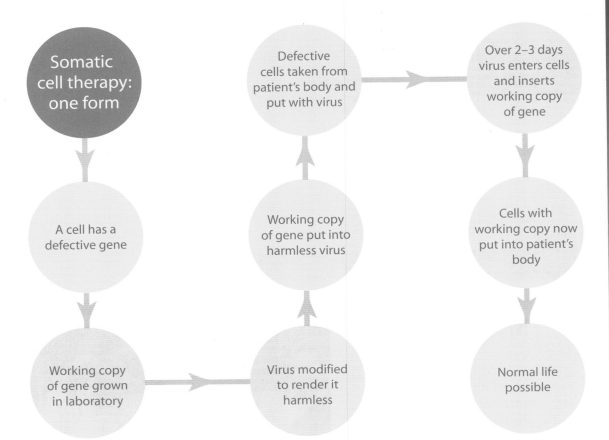

Somatic cell therapy: one form

A cell has a defective gene

→ Working copy of gene grown in laboratory

→ Virus modified to render it harmless

→ Working copy of gene put into harmless virus

→ Defective cells taken from patient's body and put with virus

→ Over 2–3 days virus enters cells and inserts working copy of gene

→ Cells with working copy now put into patient's body

→ Normal life possible

## Case study

### Rhys Evans

- Failure to respond to antibiotic treatment for infection
- Admitted to hospital
- Daily uncertainty about his survival
- Diagnosed with X-SCID
- In 2002 became first child in UK to receive somatic cell therapy
- Now a healthy schoolboy

TopFoto

## Saviour siblings

This technique is used to save the life of a child with a life-threatening disorder. In the UK, every treatment has to be approved by the HFEA. The treatment combines IVF with PGD (pre-implantation genetic diagnosis), which is a form of genetic screening. If a baby is born free from the disorder, its cord blood can be used to treat the sick sibling.

| Saviour siblings: the process | → | IVF is used to produce embryos that are then screened for signs of the disorder | → | Embryos free from the disorder and a close match with the sick child are selected for insertion into the woman |

Stem cells from the baby's cord blood are transplanted into the sick sibling ← If pregnancy follows, a child is born free from the disorder and with the prospect of a healthy life

## Case study

### Adam and Molly Nash

- Molly Nash was born with a genetic disorder that would lead to an early death
- Her parents wanted another child — but one free from the disorder
- They also wanted treatment for Molly
- Through a combination of IVF and PGD Mrs Nash conceived and gave birth to Adam, a healthy baby free from the disorder
- The stem cells from his cord blood were used to give Molly a bone marrow transplant, which was a success

Reuters

The Nash family

## Designer babies

What is lawful in the UK:

- Saviour siblings are a kind of designer baby, since their genetic make-up is selected to be as close as possible to that of the the sick sibling.
- The use of sex selection where there is a sex-linked genetic disorder.

What is not lawful in the UK:

- Sex selection for social reasons.
- Research into ways of enabling couples to choose the appearance, intellectual or sporting potential of children.

Parents should have the right to choose treatments for their children

It is a compassionate response to disease

Somatic cell therapy is just an extension of everyday treatment

It may well be more effective and less expensive than current treatments

## Arguments for human genetic engineering

The benefits outweigh any risks

Providing the saviour sibling is wanted for him/herself, saving life is good and the baby is not being harmed in any way

It saves lives

Enhancement gene therapy could prevent psychological problems associated with genetic traits

It is unnatural — medical scientists are 'playing God'

There are big risks — a French boy treated in a similar way to Rhys Evans developed leukaemia

There is fear of the slippery slope — what starts as somatic cell therapy might lead eventually to eugenics

## Arguments against human genetic engineering

'Designer babies' could become big business and it might be that only the rich could afford this, which would be an injustice

Saviour siblings might grow up to feel unwanted or that they were a means to an end. If the treatment failed, there might be disastrous psychological effects or consequences for family relationships

Some treatments might be controversial, e.g. if a gay gene were isolated and could be removed

# Religious views on human genetic engineering

 **Buddhism**

- Intentions of gene therapy are good
- Goes against First Precept if animals are used at the research stage
- Serious **kammic consequences** as a result of any alteration of human nature

 **Christianity**

### For

- Somatic cell therapy and saviour siblings save life — uphold **sanctity of life** principle
- Act of compassion
- Responsible use of God-given skills
- Extension of Jesus' healing ministry
- Can't put a price on the life of a child

### Against

- 'Playing God'
- Desire for designer babies is **idolatry**, i.e. worship of beauty, intellect etc.
- IVF treatment (see page 23) breaches sanctity of life principle
- Spending huge sums of money on very rare conditions is not good stewardship

 **Hinduism**

### For

- Somatic cell therapy and saviour siblings save life

### Against

- Genetic engineering is refusal to accept **karmic consequences** of previous existence

 **Islam**

### For

- Somatic cell therapy and saviour siblings save lives
- Saving one person's life is like saving the whole of humanity
- Responsible use of Allah's gifts

### Against

- Interfering with Allah's purposes for humans
- Only Allah has right to determine someone's genetic code

# Judaism

**For**

- Somatic cell therapy and saviour siblings relieve suffering and save lives
- Benefits outweigh risks and costs

**Against**

- 'Playing God'
- Pushing boundaries of human life
- Creation of 'designer babies' is idolatrous

# Sikhism

- Somatic cell therapy and saviour siblings save lives
- Reject concept of 'designer babies'

**Key words**

designer babies

genetic engineering

idolatry

kammic/karmic consequences

sanctity of life

saviour siblings

## Test yourself

## Case study

# The Masterson family

- Mr and Mrs Masterson wanted permission to have IVF and PGD in order to select the sex of their next child
- They already had four young sons
- Their only daughter had been killed in an accident
- They wanted another child, but did not want another boy
- Permission was refused because the selection was for social reasons
- Sex selection is permitted only when it is to prevent serious genetic conditions from being passed on

1 Give two reasons why some religious believers might agree with sex selection in the Mastersons' case.
2 Give two reasons why some religious believers might disagree with it.
3 Why might many religious believers agree with the development and use of somatic cell therapy?
4 Why might some religious believers oppose it?

# Embryology

Embryos created for IVF (see page 23) may be used for research purposes. Since 2001, research into stem-cell cloning has been allowed, together with embryonic research aimed at solving reproductive problems. There are strict rules on this:

- All research has to be licensed and is regulated by the Human Fertilisation and Embryology Authority (HFEA). Embryonic research is permitted only if there is no alternative.
- The consent of both parents is needed.
- Research may be carried out only up to 14 days after an embryo was created, which is when the nervous system starts to form. After this embryos must be destroyed.

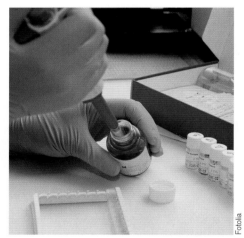

Embryos created for IVF may be used for research purposes

## Religious views on embryonic research

Religious views on **embryology** vary, but all religions oppose creating embryos just for research.

### Buddhism

**For**

- Importance of right intention
- Caring for the sick is a good intention
- Ending suffering is a way of applying **skilful means** (combination of metta, karuna and wisdom)
- Embryo not fully embodied person so few kammic consequences

**Against**

- Life begins at conception
- Embryo possesses all five **skandhas** (categories that make up individual experience)
- Breach of the **First Precept** (not to cause harm to any living thing)

## Christianity

**For**

- Embryos are potential humans so not breaking the commandment: do not kill
- Leads to saving lives — act of compassion
- Strict regulations prevent abuse

**Against**

- Right to life from conception
- Embryo has right to be treated with respect and not to be exploited
- Breaks commandment not to kill — effectively murder

## Hinduism

- Sanctity of all life
- Breaches principle of **ahimsa** (respect for life)

## Islam

**For**

- **Ensoulment** not until 40–120 days (some debate on specific time)
- No sanctity of life for embryo that has not entered woman's body
- Wasteful to destroy unwanted spare embryos
- Good use of skills given by Allah
- Leads to saving of life

**Against**

- Some believe that meaningful life begins right from conception
- Concerns about possible abuses of technology

## Judaism

- Saving life important
- Embryos outside the womb to be shown respect, but are not people

# Sikhism

- Embryo a person right from conception
- To be treated with respect
- Spare IVF embryos donated to research acceptable as long as purpose is therapeutic

**Key words**

| | |
|---|---|
| ahimsa | First Precept |
| embryology | skandhas |
| ensoulment | skilful means |

## Cloning

**Cloning** consists of creating a genetically identical copy of an organism. As a result of the successful cloning of Dolly the sheep, the attention of some medical scientists turned to humans.

Dolly the sheep, the first successful mammal clone

TopFoto

## Reproductive cloning

**Reproductive cloning** is aimed at creating human life.

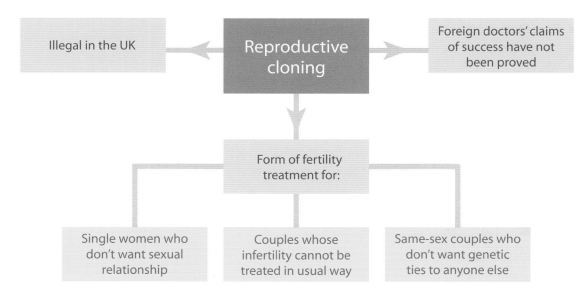

- Illegal in the UK
- **Reproductive cloning**
- Foreign doctors' claims of success have not been proved

Form of fertility treatment for:
- Single women who don't want sexual relationship
- Couples whose infertility cannot be treated in usual way
- Same-sex couples who don't want genetic ties to anyone else

## Stem cell (therapeutic) cloning

**Stem cell (therapeutic) cloning** is aimed at researching ways into curing a wide variety of diseases (e.g. motor neurone, Alzheimer's) and conditions (e.g. spinal injuries). It may only be carried out in institutes licensed by the Human Fertilisation and Embryology Act **(HFEA)** and the embryos must be destroyed at 14 days. It studies how:

- embryonic stem cells (which are pluripotent) become specialised cells
- cells become diseased

Bestselling author Terry Pratchett was diagnosed with Alzheimer's in 2007. He has made substantial donations to research into the disease

| Therapeutic cloning: the process | → | The nucleus is removed from a donated human egg | → | A nucleus from an adult cell is inserted into the empty egg |
| --- | --- | --- | --- | --- |
| The embryo is destroyed | ← | At 6 days the stem cells are removed from the blastocyst for research | ← | An electrical charge triggers it into becoming an embryo |

 **Case study**

# Christopher Reeve (1952–2004)

- A very gifted man
  - actor
  - sportsman
  - pianist
  - author
  - public speaker
- His most famous acting role was in the *Superman* films
- Political activist
  - environmental issues
  - protested against the Vietnam War
  - protested against Pinochet's death warrants against actors in Chile
  - involved with Amnesty International and Save the Children

The Superman films were highly successful

- Falling from a horse caused severe spinal cord injuries
- Totally dependent on others for washing, moving etc.
- On a ventilator until he received a new treatment in 2003
- Worked to raise awareness in USA about spinal cord injuries
- Lobbied for ending ban on funding embryonic stem cell research in USA
  - believed it would lead to successful treatment for injuries like his
  - made it a high profile campaign

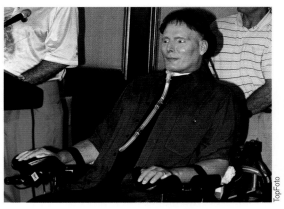

Embryonic stem cell research may lead to successful treatment for spinal cord injuries

## Religious views on cloning

### Buddhism

**For**

- Embryo does not possess five skandhas so therapeutic cloning does not break First Precept
- Importance of intention — acceptable if motivation is right

**Against**

- A living being, so breaks First Precept
- Theft of genetic material, so breaks **Second Precept** (not to steal)
- Leads to suffering, since craving lies behind decision for cloning

### Christianity

**For**

- Embryo only potential person so therapeutic cloning not tantamount to murder
- Therapeutic cloning intended to save lives — responsible use of God-given intelligence and skills
- Therapeutic cloning is an act of compassion and mercy

**Against**

- All oppose reproductive cloning as destroying the uniqueness of the individual
- Idolatrous to desire a copy of oneself

- Exploitation of embryo
- A child should be seen as a gift, not a commodity
- Playing God and could have disastrous psychological and social results
- Enormous risks — many unsuccessful attempts at animal cloning and Dolly the sheep aged prematurely
- Embryo has right to life from conception so therapeutic cloning also wrong
- Embryo has right to be treated with respect and not to be exploited
- Breaks commandment not to kill — effectively murder

 ## Hinduism

### For

- Reproductive cloning acceptable if only way to overcome infertility
- Cloned body could help atman achieve **moksha** (final freedom from **samsara**)
- Therapeutic cloning acceptable if intention good — **karma** (law of cause and effect) would not be affected

### Against

- Reproductive cloning means that copy of original still living after latter's death, so samsara (cycle of life and death) interfered with
- Suffering caused to animals and embryos at research stage for both types of cloning breaches principle of ahimsa

 ## Islam

### For

- Therapeutic cloning to treat people and save lives will be rewarded by Allah
- No moral status for embryo before 120 days

### Against

- All Muslims are against reproductive cloning as idolatrous
- Committing **shirk** (sin of claiming equality with Allah), as it is assuming role of Allah as creator
- Treats the embryo as a disposable commodity
- Confuses genetic heritage
- Threatens status of men — might no longer be needed for reproduction
- Injustice and discrimination if controlled by rich and powerful
- Some oppose therapeutic cloning because embryo fully a person from conception

# Judaism

**For**

- Reproductive cloning is a fulfilment of God's command in Genesis 1:28
- Therapeutic cloning is a use of God-given skills
- Also saving life

**Against**

- Reproductive cloning is a **blasphemous** challenge to God's authority as source of all life
- Denies uniqueness of each individual
- Injustice if controlled by those with money and possibly leading to a two-tier society
- Risk of damaged clones being born — how would they be treated?

# Sikhism

**For**

- Compassion for infertile — reproductive cloning
- Saving life — therapeutic cloning

**Against**

- Playing God — reproductive cloning is an act of interference with God's role as creator
- Concern about possible effects on rebirth

| Key words |
| --- |
| blasphemous |
| cloning |
| HFEA |
| karma |
| moksha |
| reproductive cloning |
| stem cell (therapeutic) cloning |
| samsara |
| Second Precept |
| shirk |

## Test yourself

I can't understand why people are against embryonic stem cell cloning. It could lead to cures for so many illnesses and to being able to repair organ damage. It could help paralysed people walk again, just like Jesus cured a paralysed man. So many people could have a better quality of life.

But it's not just about quality of life. What about sanctity of life? In stem cell research, embryos are created and then killed. What respect for human life does that show? And eventually someone will use the same technology to create human clones. Just because scientists can do something, it doesn't mean they should — there are limits to what they should do.

1 Explain the different purposes of reproductive and therapeutic cloning.
2 Explain why some religious believers are against therapeutic cloning.
3 Explain why some religious believers support therapeutic cloning.

## Examination question

**Explain why many religious believers oppose reproductive cloning. Refer to one or more religions in your answer.** *(6 marks)*

### Exam tip

When answering a question on embryonic research, do not confuse it with IVF or PEJD.

# Blood transfusions and organ transplants

Transplants, whatever type they are, mean putting a 'foreign body' into a person, e.g. blood, kidney, heart. There are a number of practical issues, including:

- rejection, which is dealt with by ensuring a good match and, in the case of transplanted tissue and organs, by anti-rejection drugs
- spread of disease, which is minimised by careful screening before the donation is made

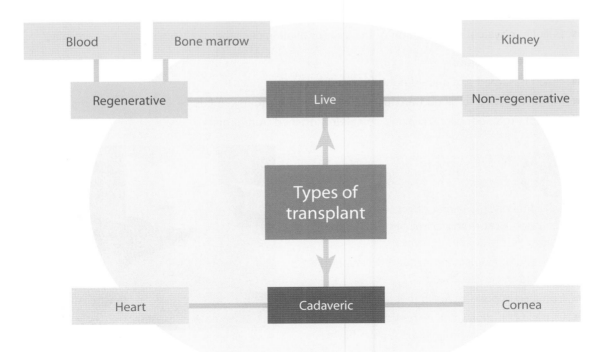

# Religious views on blood transfusions and organ transplants

## Buddhism

- Donation is a matter for individual conscience
- Fits in with the First Precept, sanctity of life, **metta** (loving kindness), **karuna** (compassion) and generosity to others
- The body is only a shell, so donating organs at death creates no kammic consequences

## Christianity

**All mainstream denominations and most individuals**
- Acts of compassion
- Jesus said that giving one's life for a friend was the supreme demonstration of love
- All forms are selfless acts of saving life
- Cadaveric donations bring good out of evil and comfort to the bereaved
- Use of God-given surgical and medical skills
- Donation is act of responsible decision-making
- Personal **autonomy** to be respected — no pressure to donate

**Some literalist Christians**
- Against organ donation
- Belief in **physical resurrection** of the body at death means that the body should be kept intact

**Jehovah's Witnesses**
- Blood is sacred and should not be passed to another
- Totally opposed to blood transfusions whatever the circumstances
- Accept organ donations if blood completely drained from organ

## Hinduism

- Individual decisions and often seen as achieving **Brahman**'s purposes (the reality from which everything comes)
- Principle of ahimsa can support donation as sick and dying are saved
- Can also oppose as live donor might be harmed
- Depends on motivation — reluctance to accept death and prolong life indefinitely not a good thing

Blood donation is an act of compassion supported by most religions

## ☪ ★ Islam

- Blood donation is encouraged as free and selfless gift
- To save one person's life is like saving humanity
- Relieving a Muslim's suffering rewarded with less suffering for donor after death (**Hadith**)
- Consent to be free and informed
- Donation to be free gift to prevent exploitation and greed
- Because of belief in physical resurrection, some concerned about physical mutilation preventing a donor's body being buried intact
- **Shari'ah law** — if two principles conflict, choose the lesser of two evils, i.e. saving a life is to take priority
- Minority opposed to organ donation on grounds that all bodies belong to Allah with no right to give what they do not own

## ✡ Judaism

- Giving blood a **mitzvah** (religious obligation)
- Life sacred
- To save one life is to save humankind, so most support organ donation
- What helps one person and does not harm another should be allowed (Talmud)
- Cadaveric transplant problematic for some — mutilates the body and burial
- Heart transplants break Sixth Commandment for those who believe death occurs when breathing and beating of heart are stopped irreversibly

## ☬ Sikhism

- All forms of donation save life and are an act of kindness
- Donation helps progress towards **mukti** (liberation from cycle of rebirth)
- Form of **sewa** (service)
- No problem with cadaveric donation as body just a shell and no rules about burial
- Gift must be free

## Experiments on humans

After testing on animals, new medical treatments have to be tested on humans before they can come onto the market. They are governed by rules found in the Declaration of Helsinki, covering:
- the use of vulnerable people (e.g. children)
- the importance of informed consent

There are few specific religious concerns providing that:
- procedures are carried out carefully
- the safety of volunteers and patients comes before money to be made or cost-cutting concerns

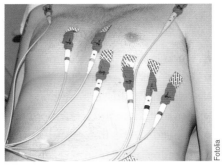
Testing on humans is carried out under strict rules

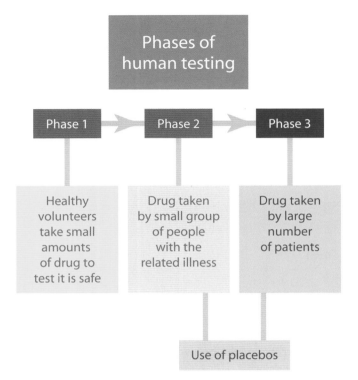

**Phases of human testing**

Phase 1 → Phase 2 → Phase 3

| Phase 1 | Phase 2 | Phase 3 |
|---|---|---|
| Healthy volunteers take small amounts of drug to test it is safe | Drug taken by small group of people with the related illness | Drug taken by large number of patients |

Use of placebos

**Key words**

autonomy
blood transfusion
Brahman
Hadith
karuna
metta
mitzvah
mukti
physical resurrection
sewa
Shari'ah law

## Test yourself

1 Fill in each of the gaps with the correct word:

Sometimes a person needs a blood t............................. It is very important to get the blood group right to ensure a perfect m............................. Almost all religious believers encourage people to become blood donors, as it is a k............................. act and leads to lives being s............................. There are two main types of transplant surgery. One involves l............................. donation of an organ or tissue. For instance, sometimes a relative gives a k............................. to s............................. life. The other type is when a person has died; this is known as c............................. donation. For instance, the relatives of someone who has been killed in a road accident might agree to organs such as the h............................. or l............................. being donated.

2 Explain the attitudes of religious believers towards transplant surgery. Refer to one or more religion(s) in your answer.

## Examination question

**1 Explain briefly why some religious believers might not wish to donate blood.**  *(2 marks)*

**2 Describe briefly the three phases involved in experiments on humans.**  *(2 marks)*

### Exam tip

The command words 'describe briefly' or 'explain briefly' are used in questions that do not require as much detail. They often require one or two points with slight development.

# Fertility treatments

**Infertility** is caused by a variety of factors. Sometimes the problem can be solved, but often couples have to resort to particular types of **fertility treatment**. The distress caused by infertility has been compared to that caused by bereavement: it is intense and long-lasting, if not permanent. It creates a sense of inadequacy, failure and emptiness. The Old Testament story of Hannah (1 Samuel 1) illustrates the effects.

Her husband…would ask her: 'Hannah, why are you crying? Why won't you eat? Why are you always so sad? Don't I mean more to you than ten sons?' (1 Samuel 1:8)

## Methods of treatment

### AIH:

- the husband's/partner's sperm is collected and inserted into the woman's vagina; fertilisation is left to occur naturally

### AID/DI:

- as for AIH, but with the use of donors who have been paid a small sum to donate sperm to a donor bank; the husband's name appears on the birth certificate, but when they reach 18 children have the right to know the identity of their genetic fathers

### IVF:

- hormonal treatment increases the number of eggs that ripen; at maturity they are collected and put in a dish, to be fertilised with the sperm that has also been collected; after checks for viability one or two embryos are put into the uterus

IVF
(in vitro fertilisation)

Fertility treatments

AIH
(artificial insemination by husband)

AID/DI
(artificial insemination by donor/donor insemination)

- spare embryos may be frozen for up to ten years; they may be used for future cycles of treatment, donated to other infertile couples or donated for **embryonic research**; otherwise they are destroyed
- both partners must agree about the use of any spare embryos

Embryologist freezing embryos for storage

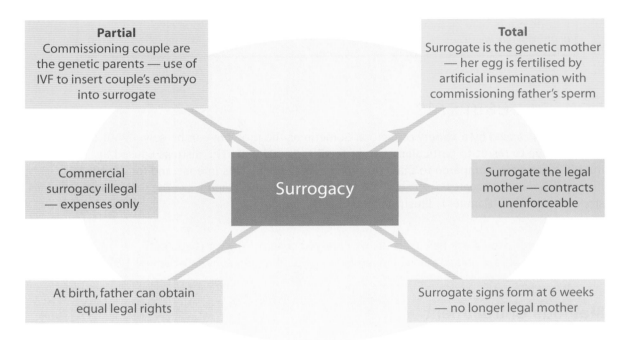

**Partial**
Commissioning couple are the genetic parents — use of IVF to insert couple's embryo into surrogate

**Total**
Surrogate is the genetic mother — her egg is fertilised by artificial insemination with commissioning father's sperm

Commercial surrogacy illegal — expenses only

Surrogacy

Surrogate the legal mother — contracts unenforceable

At birth, father can obtain equal legal rights

Surrogate signs form at 6 weeks — no longer legal mother

## Religious views on fertility treatments

 **Buddhism**

**For**

- Use of IVF matter for individual choice
- Shows metta and karuna and promotes sanctity of life
- Fulfilling duty to use skilful means

**Against**

- Production of spare embryos disrespectful of life
- Kammic implications
- Potential social and psychological problems with donor treatments and surrogacy

# ✚ Christianity

## Protestants

- Children are a blessing
- Compassionate to infertile
- Right use of God-given medical skills
- Extension of Jesus' healing ministry
- Putting nature right
- Some are concerned about possible psychological problems with donor treatment and surrogacy; others see it as a particularly selfless form of treatment
- Concern about social and psychological problems arising out of surrogacy and possible exploitation of surrogacy

## Roman Catholics

- Children are a gift from God — infertility to be accepted as God's will
- Against natural law, which states that children should be produced by an act that is **unitive** and **procreative**
- Donor treatments and surrogacy are a form of '**mechanical adultery**' and create social and psychological problems
- Creation of spare embryos disrespects life

 Hinduism

- Important to have children
- Many accept AIH and some support IVF providing sperm comes from husband
- Child's caste traced through male ancestry so donor insemination unacceptable
- Donor treatments and surrogacy seen as forms of **adultery**

 Islam

## Majority view

- Children are an important part of marriage
- Medical skills given by Allah
- Accept AIH and IVF if sperm is from husband but not from a dead or divorced partner
- Donor treatments and surrogacy are a form of adultery
- The mother of a child is the one who gives birth (Qur'an)

## Minority view

- 'Playing God' — Allah gives life and chooses who will have children
- Infertility is a test of faith to be accepted as Allah's will
- **Polygamy** is an alternative to infertility in Islamic countries

# Judaism

### Orthodox Jews

- Life is a gift from God so no fertilisation outside the body
- Masturbation is sinful — it 'wastes seed' — rules out fertility treatments
- Donor treatments and surrogacy are tantamount to adultery
- Surrogacy has potential social and psychological problems
  — child's religious identity comes from mother

### Reform Jews

- Same views as Orthodox Jews about donated eggs and sperm
- Acceptance of AIH and IVF as long as sperm comes from husband
  — sperm not 'wasted seed' since being put to good use

# Sikhism

- Some think infertility to be accepted as God's will
- Most see assisted conception as matter for conscience
- Many accept AIH and IVF where sperm comes from husband
- Donor treatments tantamount to adultery and might make infertile partner feel inadequate
- Surrogacy is unnatural

| Key words |
| --- |
| adultery |
| AID/DI |
| AIH |
| embryonic research |
| fertility treatment |
| infertility |
| IVF |
| mechanical adultery |
| Orthodox Jews |
| polygamy |
| procreative |
| Reform Jews |
| surrogacy |
| unitive |

## *Test yourself*

 **Case study**

## Kim Cotton and COTS

- She was the UK's first commercial surrogate mother and was paid £6,500
- She then sold her story for a huge sum to a newspaper
- She provided the egg, which was inseminated with the commissioning father's sperm
- She has never had any contact with the child or the parents and still finds this hard
- She later carried a child (without a fee) for an infertile friend and the relationship is still close
- She founded COTS (Childlessness Overcome through Surrogacy) as a non-profit-making introduction agency for surrogates and infertile couples

Kim Cotton

- She left (though is still a patron) because of a series of scandals, e.g. large sums of money being paid to surrogates, surrogates refusing to hand the child over or having abortions, commissioning parents not wanting the child after it was born
- She is still convinced of the value of surrogacy and claims that mostly it works out well for the surrogates, the parents, the children
- She prefers partial (host surrogacy) as that creates fewer emotional problems for the surrogate

1 Give three arguments in favour of surrogacy.
2 Give three arguments against surrogacy.
3 Explain why some religious believers disagree with the use of IVF.
4 Explain why some religious believers accept the use of IVF.

## Examination question

**'Religious believers should never become surrogate mothers.'**

**What do you think? Explain your opinion.** *(3 marks)*

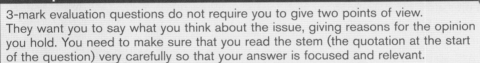

### Exam tip

3-mark evaluation questions do not require you to give two points of view. They want you to say what you think about the issue, giving reasons for the opinion you hold. You need to make sure that you read the stem (the quotation at the start of the question) very carefully so that your answer is focused and relevant.

**Topic 2**

# Religious attitudes to the elderly and death

## Senior citizenship

Medical and other advances mean that the elderly can now enjoy a longer and better quality of life than in the past. Although ageism continues to be a problem, many continue to work well beyond retirement age. Others take the advantage of retirement and cheap travel to enjoy many leisure activities. There are negative aspects to greater life expectancy, however. There are increasing financial pressures on state finances and, for those elderly people who are frail, longer life in old age is not always seen as a blessing. Many old people live far from their children and so suffer from loneliness. Others are too frail to live on their own and families may not be able or want to take responsibility for them. There is a booming business in residential homes, but these vary in quality.

Many elderly people in Britain enjoy active and fulfilling lives

Being loved and wanted

Quality of life

Having capacity for relationships

Having capacity for self-fulfilled life

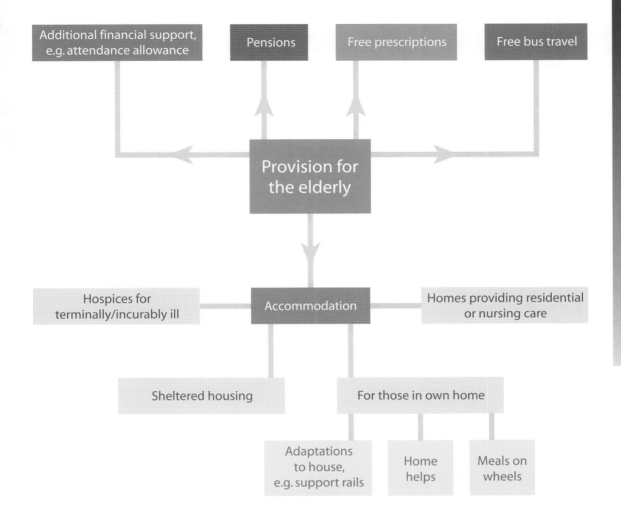

## Religious attitudes to caring for the elderly

- The elderly are respected for their wisdom and experience
- Their vulnerability is an important lesson to younger Buddhists on the **Three Marks of Existence**
- Caring for parents is the highest form of protection, a duty and the right response to the care that parents gave in the past
- Caring for the elderly builds up good kamma
- Although the elderly should be with their families until death, it might not always be possible so Buddhists work with **hospices** etc. to provide good care in such situations

## Christianity

- 'Honour your father and mother' (Fifth Commandment) reinforced in New Testament
- The vulnerable and defenceless are to be given special protection
- The elderly should feel secure in the love of their family, though it is not always possible to live with them
- If in their own home or residential care, the elderly should have regular contact with the family
- Christian churches provide for the needs of the elderly with clubs, day care centres, outings etc.
- Churches provide transport to get the elderly to church or visit them if housebound, take Holy Communion to them etc.
- Many hospices for terminally or incurably ill people have Christian foundations

## Hinduism

- Extended family central to Hindu life
- Elderly are expected to study scriptures and pass on Hindu stories to younger family members
- **Pitri jajna** (one of five daily duties) entails showing respect, fulfilling parents' wishes, seeking their advice
- Parents to be treated as gods
- Duty of oldest son is to provide home for parents and carry out set rituals at their funerals

## Islam

- Parents to be shown kindness and respect, with no harsh words (Surah 17:23–24)
- Age takes priority in family life
- Those who do not honour their parents are not part of the **ummah** (brotherhood of Muslims) and will face judgement for it (Hadith)
- Concept of extended family is important and the idea of residential homes for elderly abhorrent, though hospices may be used

## Judaism

- Honour your father and mother (Fifth Commandment)
- Idea of extended family strong in Judaism and residential homes are a last resort
- Jewish Care is a charity that runs sheltered housing, residential homes, day centres and care packages

# Sikhism

- Sinful to argue with parents (Guru Granth Sahib)
- Respect and care for elderly and sick are part of sewa
- Prayer pointless if these duties not carried out
- Elderly cared for by family members
- **Gurdwaras** (places of worship) run day-care centres and offer other forms of care to support families

## Life-support machines

The chief use of **life-support machines** is to provide short-term assistance with breathing for:
- premature or very sick babies
- people who have undergone major surgery
- those in trauma

Life-support machines may be used to assess whether or not someone is brain stem dead. Machines are switched off if the brain stem is dead. Where that is not the case, but the patient's future quality of life will be very poor, doctors and patients come to an agreed decision about whether to switch off the machine. Brain stem death is currently the accepted standard for assessing that death has occurred. Many would like this extended to include neo-cortical death: this is where the brain stem is intact but that area of the brain that provides consciousness has been irreversibly destroyed. The person therefore exists rather than lives.

## Religious views on life support

All religions accept switching off life support for brain-dead people.

### Buddhism

- Life to be respected and preserved — First Precept and principle of sanctity of life
- But might show metta and karuna to switch off life support if quality of life is going to be poor
- Motivation all-important (**Dalai Lama** — the Tibetan religious leader)
- Need to consider kammic effects of action

The Dalai Lama gives a Buddhist perspective on complex modern issues such as the right use of life-support systems

### Christianity

- Life is a sacred gift from God
- Bodies are temples of the Holy Spirit (Paul)
- Often reluctant to discontinue life support where there is hope of survival
- Anglicans promote idea of dying with dignity — letting nature take its course and allowing the person to die is the best way of showing love of neighbour

### Hinduism

- Brahman to decide the time of death
- Might mean not prolonging life artificially by life support
- Respect for life might justify life support
- Effects of karma on the patient and the person making the decision need to be considered

   ## Islam

- Principle of sanctity of life
- Unnatural life prolongation against Allah's will — nature to be allowed to take its course where certain that recovery will never occur

## Judaism

- Life is God's precious gift and to be preserved unless there is no hope of recovery

  ## Sikhism

- Life is sacred and to be preserved even when suffering
- But not to prevent nature from taking its course if there is no hope of recovery

# Religious teachings on death

## Buddhism

- Death is a stepping stone to rebirth
- Relatives perform **dana** (acts of charity) to give dying person merit
- Kamma created by great goodness or evil can carry through several rebirths
- **Nibbana** (state of perfect peace, no longer bound to samsara) achieved through enlightenment
- Cremation makes finality of death clear

## Christianity

- Dying are encouraged to trust in God's mercy and forgiveness
- Loved ones read from the Bible and pray for/with the dying person in the home and in church
- Roman Catholics and many Anglicans receive the last rites
- Practical care for both the dying and their carers
- Belief in eternal life with God after death as a result of Jesus' resurrection
- Beliefs about time of judgement vary — at death, a Judgement Day or both
- Many believe in heaven (being with God eternally) and hell (eternal separation from God)
- Some believe in universal salvation
- Belief that life after death is totally different — no suffering etc., either resurrection with a new heavenly body or immortality of soul
- Roman Catholic belief in **purgatory** — time of cleansing from sin and preparation for heaven; prayers for the dead and good deeds might shorten this period

## Hinduism

- Relatives read to dying from sacred texts and pray
- Friends offer family practical and spiritual support
- Carry out correct **samskaras** (rites) after death to ensure better reincarnation
- At death, **atman** moves on to new body — dependent on karma acquired
- Aim to escape samsara and achieve moksha — being one with Brahman
- Cremation and scattering of ashes in local river or taken to Ganges

## Islam

- Repetition of prayers, verses from the Qur'an and the **Shahadah** (Muslim declaration of faith) — Allah the last word heard by the dying
- Death is just a stage in life, not the end
- Funeral immediately after death
- Dead person asked questions by two angels
- Soul goes to **Al-barzakh** (place of waiting outside time)
- Souls united with bodies to resurrect and join living for judgement (Yawmuddin)
- Either paradise (**Al-janna**) or hell (**Jahannam**)
- Martyrs go straight to paradise

## Judaism

- Saying of **Shema** (Jewish prayer) and reading from the **Tenakh** (Jewish scriptures)
- Practical and emotional support for individual and relatives
- Especially kind deed to ensure that eyes of dead person are shut
- **Talmud** (commentary on the Torah) discourages speculation about life after death — living this life well is what matters
- Many believe in day of resurrection when the **Messiah** (God's chosen leader) comes
- Wicked go to **Gehinnom** (hell) to be cleansed from sin before enjoying peace of messianic age

A Jewish funeral at the Mount of Olives cemetery in Jerusalem

# Sikhism

- Hymns recited from Guru Granth Sahib and Sukhmani said — dying person replies with **Waheguru** ('Wonderful Lord')
- Practical and spiritual support given to family
- Soul is reborn when body dies — form taken dependent on karma acquired
- Longing for mukti — achieved through good life, meditation and worship

## *Test yourself*

1 Explain what is meant by quality of life.
2 Give three ways in which the state cares for the elderly.
3 Explain three ways in which hospices care for the terminally ill.
4 What is meant by brain death?
5 When do all religions agree with the turning off of life support machines?
6 Explain other situations when many religious believers would agree with the withdrawal of life support.

## *Examination question*

**Describe beliefs about life after death in one religion that you have studied.** *(6 marks)*

### Exam tip

The command word 'describe' requires a detailed account. Do not include explanation, as this will simply use up valuable time.

### Key words

Al-barzakh
Al-janna
atman
Dalai Lama
dana
Gehinnom
gurdwara
hospices
Jahannam
life-support machines
Messiah
Nibbana
pitri jajna
purgatory
samskaras
Shahadah
Shema
Talmud
Tenakh
Three Marks of Existence
ummah
Waheguru

# Euthanasia

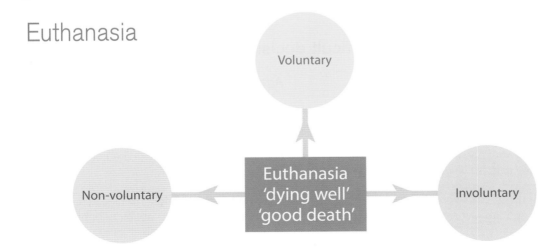

**Euthanasia** is often explained as 'mercy killing' or 'dying with dignity'.

Voluntary euthanasia refers to the request by a person for the doctor to end a life of intolerable suffering or loss of dignity.

Non-voluntary euthanasia refers to a situation where a person is incapable of making a request, e.g. is in a long-term coma or cannot communicate at all. Euthanasia is thought to be in that individual's best interests and what he/she would have wanted.

Involuntary euthanasia refers to the kind of practice that went on in Nazi Germany, where a person is put to death without being consulted and with no thought given to the best interests of that individual.

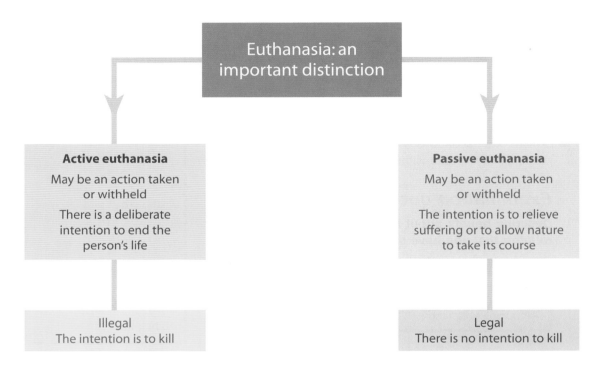

## Active euthanasia: some difficult decisions

| For | Against |
|---|---|
| The right to self-determination — it is genuinely what the patient wants | Can one be sure it is real and lasting desire? Might it be due to feelings of pressure? |
| No animal would be made to suffer continual intolerable pain, so why should a human being? | Improvements in palliative care make it unnecessary |
| Feeding tubes simply prolong the dying of PVS patients and are just a form of medical treatment | Feeding tubes are a form of basic care to which everyone has an absolute right |

## Passive euthanasia: some difficult decisions

| For | Against |
|---|---|
| Giving a high dose of morphine may shorten life, but its intention is to relieve pain | Is relief of pain the only motive in giving morphine? If not, it just prolongs the dying |
| Withholding or withdrawing treatment that has no useful purpose allows nature to take its course | Withholding or withdrawing treatment just prolongs the suffering and is cruel |
| The law protects the majority of society from harmful consequences of allowing euthanasia | Suicide is legal; not to allow disabled people help with dying from doctors is discrimination |

**Dignity in Dying**

Campaigns to legalise:

- voluntary euthanasia
- living wills

**The ProLife Alliance**

Campaigns to promote:

- the right to life as fundamental
- the provision of more hospices

Diane Pretty claimed that not allowing her to commit assisted suicide was an act of discrimination

## Case study

# Lilian Boyes and Dr Nigel Cox

- Lilian Boyes suffered from rheumatoid arthritis
- Her consultant was Dr Nigel Cox
- In 1991 she was admitted to hospital
- She was always in extreme pain and could not bear anyone to touch her or hold her hand
- She repeatedly asked Dr Cox to give her a lethal injection
- Eventually out of compassion he gave her an injection of potassium chloride, which was not a painkiller but would stop her heart
- He entered this in the hospital notes and when these were later checked, he was reported for his action
- In 1992 he was convicted of attempted murder, but was given a suspended prison sentence
- He was allowed to continue to practise medicine

# Religious teachings on voluntary euthanasia

 **Buddhism**

**For**

- Intention all-important — no negative kamma if motivated by metta and karuna
- Body just a shell for the life force

**Against**

- Goes against First Precept
- **Dukkha** (Third Mark of Existence) teaches that suffering is a part of life that should be accepted
- Dying is opportunity for spiritual development and good kamma

 **Christianity**

All Christians accept passive euthanasia

**For**

- View of some individual Christians and of most in **Dutch Protestant Church**
- Quality of life might sometimes come before absolute sanctity of life
- Total loss of dignity is not what it means to be created in the image of God and unbearable suffering is contrary to God's will — euthanasia shows compassion
- Right to and duty of responsible decision-making given by God

**Against**

- View of all mainstream UK denominations
- Life sacred and God-given and there are limits to right to autonomy — breaks Sixth Commandment
- Lack of trust in God's love and compassion
- Hospice movement and palliative care preserve human dignity better than euthanasia
- Duty to defend the vulnerable

 **Hinduism**

Passive euthanasia accepted

- Prevents performance of **dharma** (religious duty) and is contrary to ahimsa
- Should accept suffering as result of karma from previous existence — euthanasia would just create more bad karma unless intention absolutely selfless

 **Islam**

Passive euthanasia accepted — seen as submission to Allah's will

- Suffering might be Allah's plan — he knows what is best and his decisions should not be challenged
- Euthanasia causes suffering to others

# Judaism

Some Jews accept passive euthanasia as allowing God's will to be achieved

- Life is sacred and to be treasured
- God alone is the giver and taker of life
- Breaks the Sixth Commandment

# Sikhism

Passive euthanasia accepted by some

**For**

- Minority view
- If a person wishes to die and a medical condition is causing severe problems for family, it should be allowed

**Against**

- Only God should give and take life
- Suffering is part of God's plan and to be accepted as expression of God's will
- Wrong to interfere with natural course of life

| Key words |
| --- |
| active euthanasia |
| dharma |
| dukkha |
| Dutch Protestant Church |
| euthanasia |
| passive euthanasia |

## *Test yourself*

**1 True or false?**

| | TRUE | FALSE |
| --- | --- | --- |
| Voluntary euthanasia is illegal but non-voluntary euthanasia is legal in the UK. | | |
| Active euthanasia is illegal but passive euthanasia is legal in the UK. | | |
| Giving a cancer patient morphine to relieve pain, even though it will shorten the person's life, is allowed in UK law. | | |
| Dr Cox was found guilty of attempted murder when he carried out Lilian Boyes' request for euthanasia. | | |
| The Anglican Church agrees with voluntary euthanasia. | | |
| The Roman Catholic Church agrees with voluntary euthanasia. | | |
| Some individual Christians agree with voluntary euthanasia. | | |
| Many religious believers accept passive euthanasia. | | |
| Dignity in Dying is an organisation that opposes legalising voluntary euthanasia. | | |
| The ProLife Alliance opposes legalising voluntary euthanasia. | | |

**2** Explain how belief in the sanctity of life might influence a religious believer's attitude to voluntary euthanasia.

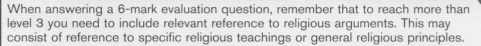

## *Examination question*

**'When people are suffering unbearable pain, voluntary euthanasia is the kindest action to take.'**

**Do you agree? Give reasons for your answer, showing that you have thought about more than one point of view. Refer to religious arguments in your answer.**                    *(6 marks)*

### Exam tip

When answering a 6-mark evaluation question, remember that to reach more than level 3 you need to include relevant reference to religious arguments. This may consist of reference to specific religious teachings or general religious principles.

# Topic 3
# Religious attitudes to drug abuse

## Types of drug and their effects

A **drug** is a natural or artificial substance that has physical and/or emotional and mental effects when taken. These effects may be beneficial or harmful. Drugs may be legal, legal when prescribed by a doctor or illegal.

Prescribed drugs
- Morphine
- Sedatives

Types of drugs

Legal social drugs
- Alcohol
- Tobacco
- Caffeine

Illegal drugs
- Heroin
- Cannabis

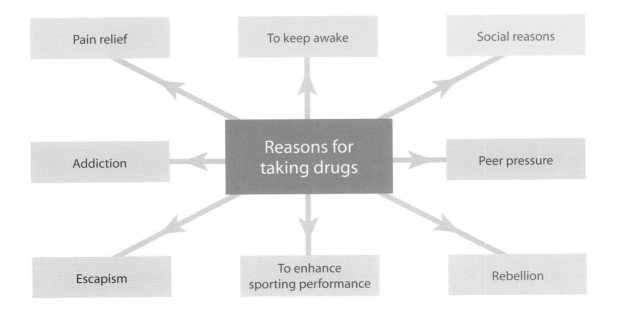

Pain relief

To keep awake

Social reasons

Addiction

Reasons for taking drugs

Peer pressure

Escapism

To enhance sporting performance

Rebellion

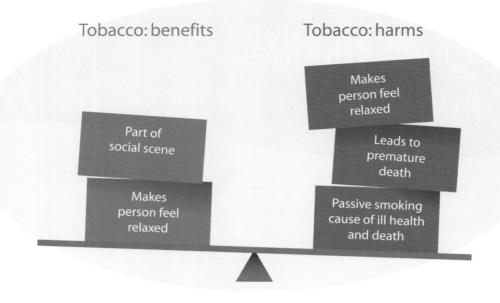

Tobacco: benefits

Tobacco: harms

Part of social scene

Makes person feel relaxed

Makes person feel relaxed

Leads to premature death

Passive smoking cause of ill health and death

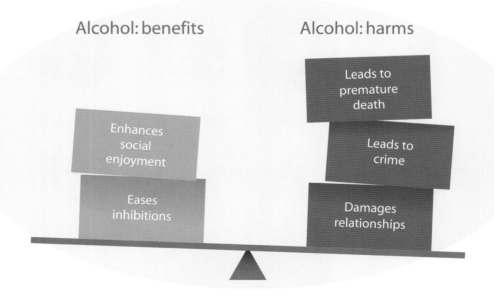

Alcohol: benefits

Alcohol: harms

Enhances social enjoyment

Eases inhibitions

Leads to premature death

Leads to crime

Damages relationships

## Social drug-taking

Despite all the highlighting in the media of the dangers of smoking and heavy drinking, both continue to be a serious problem and they account for a significant proportion of public expenditure, particularly in the health service. Government thinking seems to be that increasing taxes on **tobacco** and **alcohol** will make people give up smoking and cut down on drinking. Many people would like to see these taxes used in education and in the National Health Service.

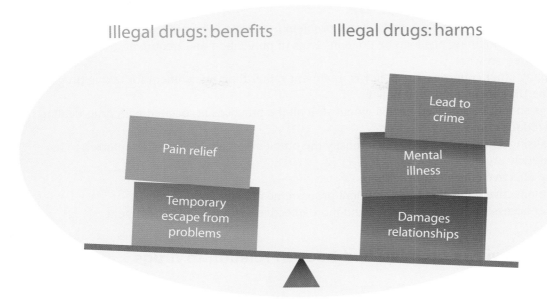

Illegal drugs: benefits

Illegal drugs: harms

Pain relief

Temporary escape from problems

Lead to crime

Mental illness

Damages relationships

Classification and legal status of drugs

Class A: most harmful and addictive, e.g. **heroin**, **ecstasy**. Severe penalties for dealing and quite severe for possession

Class B: can be very harmful, e.g. amphetamines, **cannabis**. Severe penalties for dealing and quite severe for possession

Class C: can be harmful, e.g. tranquillisers. Severe penalties for dealing but less severe for possession

**Solvents**: not illegal, but shops not allowed to sell them to those under 18

## Illegal drug-taking in the UK

The UK has the most serious illegal drugs problem in Europe. While the general public is agreed that something needs to be done in terms of prevention and treatment, even experts do not agree on what.

- In many other countries, the policy is treatment rather than punishment for taking drugs, so the UK should adopt that policy
- Drugs should be legalised as this would stop all the practices associated with drug-dealing, and reduce crime
- Legalising soft drugs would only intensify the problem — cannabis is often referred to as a gateway drug
- More effective education in schools
- More effective education and treatment programmes in prisons
- Better access to treatment centres and more effective follow-up after treatment

## Religious views on mind and body in relation to drugs

 **Buddhism**

- Human life is the perfect/very precious rebirth (Tibetan Buddhism)
- Living according to **magga** (Middle Way) and using meditation includes taking care of bodies to enhance spiritual life
- First Precept about not harming anyone — social and illegal drugs may cause harm to self, others and environment
- **Fifth Precept** (not to take intoxicants that cloud the mind) cuts out social and illegal drugs
- Kammic consequences
- Only medicinal drugs are acceptable
- Practice of right livelihood cuts out any involvement in production of non-medicinal drugs
- Right action cuts out use of performance-enhancing drugs in sport
- Involvement in drug treatment centres as expression of metta and karuna

 **Christianity**

- Human body and mind are priceless gifts from God (Psalm 8:4–5; Psalm 139:13; Luke 12:6–7)
- Body to be respected as temple of Holy Spirit
- Most Christians discourage smoking because of harm it does and because not good **stewardship** of money
- Attitudes vary about alcohol

| Majority view | Salvation Army and many Methodists |
|---|---|
| Acceptable in moderation — heavy drinking causes many problems and makes people loud and foolish (Proverbs 20:1) | **Teetotal** — sets bad example to others |
| Given by God to give joy to humans (Psalm 104) | Breaks up families |
| Jesus drank and he used wine at institution of **Holy Communion** | Leads to crime and causes accidents etc. |
| Christian treatment centres, soup kitchens etc. for alcoholics | Salvation Army hostels |

- All mainstream denominations are against the use of illegal drugs — cause of immense harm to self, family and society
- Shows disrespect to body and mind
- The new slavery (Pope John Paul II)
- Use of performance-enhancing drugs is dishonest
- Duty to obey law of land (Romans 13)
- **Rastafarians** justify use of **marijuana** (ganja weed) — God gave herbs and plants to be used (Genesis 1:12, 29)
- Compassion for drug addicts following Jesus' example (Mark 2:17) and shown practically and through prayer

## Yeldall Bridges

- A Christian centre providing residential rehabilitation for men aged 18–50 with serious drug or alcohol problems
- The initial programme lasts 3–6 months and includes:
  - individual and group therapy
  - learning about life skills, attitudes etc.
  - recreation, e.g. sport
  - daily work in the house or grounds
  - further skills training, e.g. literacy and numeracy, food hygiene
- The second stage lasts 3–4 months
- Residents live in flats and prepare for independent living
- After completing the programme there is aftercare for up to a year

Yeldall Bridges has been helping men to overcome serious drug or alcohol addictions

 **Hinduism**

- Idea of balance in bodily systems leads to use of **ayurvedic treatments** along with modern medicine to serve the atman
- Harming body creates negative karma
- Principle of ahimsa and goal of moksha — many Hindus oppose smoking, drinking and illegal drugs
- In India smoking is banned in many public places and alcohol is not served at government functions
- Not to become dependent on drugs (**laws of Manu**)
- Many Hindus smoke and drink in moderation but reject illegal drugs because of potential dangers
- **Sadhus** (holy men) use alcohol and cannabis in meditation

 **Islam**

- Role as **khalifahs** (stewards) entails treating body as a temple and keeping mind alert for prayer
- Acceptance of medicinal drugs if necessary, including those that contain alcohol if no alternative
- To avoid anything that would lead to destruction (Qur'an)
- To avoid hurting self or neighbour (Hadith)
- Smoking **makruh** (disapproved of) but not **haram** (forbidden)
- Smoking not allowed during **Ramadan** or near other people
- Alcohol haram (**surah** 5:93–94) — flogging is Shari'ah punishment
- Seen as the mother of all vices and one of **Iblis'** most effective temptations
- Muhammad stated that those who drank were not believers
- Alcohol also **khamr** — makes mind unfit to concentrate on Allah's will
- May not pray in mosque for 40 days after drinking and can only pray anywhere if mind is totally clear
- Not to sell alcohol, own or work in place that sells it or give it as present
- Any involvement with illegal drugs is haram because of harm caused and it breaks the law
- Illegal drugs khamr — same restrictions on prayer and same Shari'ah penalty
- Muslims are expected to help addicts

### A Muslim cautionary tale

A man was asked to choose between ripping the Qur'an, killing a child, worshipping an idol, drinking a cup of wine or having sex with a woman (not his wife). He decided that drinking the wine would be the least evil, so he drank it and then went on to do all the other things!

# Judaism

- Humans created in God's image — treat minds and bodies with respect
- Keeping body fit and healthy is a way of serving God (**Maimonides**)
- Use of medicinal drugs allowed
- Many Jews discourage smoking (especially in public places and on **Shabbat**) because bodies are on loan from God
- Drinking makes people loud and foolish (Proverbs 20:1)
- Rabbi cannot give ruling if he/she has had a glass of wine (Talmud)
- Wine brings joy (Psalm 104) and is used on Shabbat and **Pesach**
- Encouragement to drink too much at **Purim** (Talmud)
- Totally opposed to use of illegal drugs
- **Halakhic rules** forbid breaking law of land, losing self-control, harming bodies
- Care given to addicts and alcoholics

It is customary to drink wine, share food and wear costumes during the Jewish Purim festival

 # Sikhism

- Bodies to be respected as temples made by God
- Strong emphasis on physical fitness
- **Kesh** is a symbol of faith and commitment and keeping body in natural state
- **Kangha** is a symbol of cleanliness
- Mind to be kept clear to focus on God
- **Kurahits** (prohibitions) in **Reht Maryada** (code of conduct) ban use of tobacco, alcohol and illegal drugs — those who break them have to undergo **Khalsa** (community of the pure) initiation again
- **Nihang Sikhs** take cannabis to help with meditation
- Many work with addicts as form of sewa

Sikhs use a comb, or kangha, to secure their hair before winding on the turban

## Key words

- alcohol
- ayurvedic treatments
- caffeine
- cannabis
- drug
- ecstasy
- Fifth Precept
- gurus
- halakhic rules
- haram
- heroin
- Holy Communion
- Iblis
- kangha
- kesh
- khalifahs
- Khalsa
- khamr
- kurahits
- laws of Manu
- magga
- Maimonides
- makruh
- marijuana
- Nihang Sikhs
- Pesach
- Purim
- Ramadan
- Rastafarians
- Reht Maryada
- sadhus
- Shabbat
- solvents
- stewardship
- surah
- teetotal
- tobacco

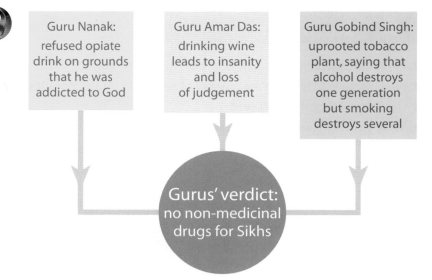

**Guru Nanak:** refused opiate drink on grounds that he was addicted to God

**Guru Amar Das:** drinking wine leads to insanity and loss of judgement

**Guru Gobind Singh:** uprooted tobacco plant, saying that alcohol destroys one generation but smoking destroys several

**Gurus' verdict:** no non-medicinal drugs for Sikhs

## *Test yourself*

## Case study

## Jackie Pullinger

- She wanted to become a missionary and in 1966, aged 22, she went to Hong Kong
- She became a primary teacher in the Walled City, the most deprived and dangerous part of Kowloon
- She opened a small youth club
- Many who came were members of Triad gangs and drug addicts
- Some became Christian and overcame their addiction
- She gave up her teaching job to concentrate on working with young people
- She opened a home for those who needed help
- She won the respect of one Triad leader who promised not to hound any of the members of his gang who left through becoming Christian
- She and two missionaries have set up St Stephen's Society, a drug rehabilitation programme in Hong Kong and Southeast Asia

1 Explain how Jackie Pullinger's beliefs led her to work with drug addicts and Triad members in Hong Kong. Include references to Christian teachings in your answer.

2 Complete the four boxes in the diagram below by giving four effects of alcohol misuse.

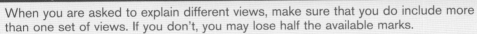

<table>
<tr><td>[ ]</td><td></td><td>[ ]</td></tr>
</table>

Effects of alcohol misuse

## Examination question

**Explain why religious believers hold different views on drinking alcohol. Refer to at least one religion in your answer.** *(6 marks)*

**Exam tip**

When you are asked to explain different views, make sure that you do include more than one set of views. If you don't, you may lose half the available marks.

# Topic 4
# Religious attitudes to crime and punishment

## Crime and punishment

| | | |
|---|---|---|
| May also be crimes, e.g. adultery in Islamic countries | Religious offences (sins) | May not be crime, e.g. adultery in the UK |

**Types of offence**

| | | |
|---|---|---|
| e.g. theft | | e.g. murder |
| Against property | Crimes (offences against a country's law) | Against the person |
| e.g. selling state secrets | Against the state | e.g. terrorism |

## Explanations for crime

There are many views on what is at the root of crime. The fundamental causes are:

- social
- environmental
- psychological
- a mixture of one or more of the above

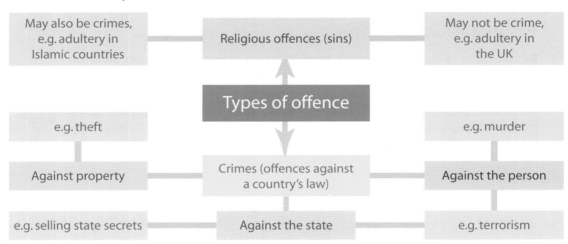

| | | |
|---|---|---|
| Alcohol and drugs | Poverty | Boredom |
| Greed | **Causes of crime** | Upbringing |
| Peer pressure | Protest | Emotional state |

# Forms of punishment

There are many different types of punishment that a judge or magistrate can give an offender. When deciding on a sentence, the offender's past history is taken into account, along with any mitigating circumstances and the seriousness of the offence. There are particular concerns with the handling of young offenders. Many feel that a custodial sentence should rarely be given and that, if it is, addressing the underlying reasons for the offence and giving the young person effective help should be priorities.

### Imprisonment

■ There are four categories of adult **prison**, ranging from high security for offenders who might pose a threat to society (A) to open prisons for those nearing the end of a sentence or who are not dangerous.

■ The conditions in many prisons are very bad:
  – overcrowding and poor sanitation
  – lack of opportunity for education and work training
  – bullying
  – being locked up for almost the whole day

■ Young people who need to be kept in custody may be put in:
  – young offender institutions
  – secure training centres
  – local authority secure children's homes

■ Adult prisoners who have behaved well in prison, who show signs of remorse and who are unlikely to pose a threat to society may be given **parole**, which involves early release with monitoring by a parole officer and sometimes **electronic tagging**.

TopFoto

Imprisonment is just one type of punishment that can be given to offenders

### Probation

Offenders are under the supervision of a **probation** officer for a set period of time. They meet up regularly to discuss progress.

### Community service

Offenders have to carry out unpaid work that benefits the community in their own time for a set period of hours.

### Fines

These are sums of money paid to the court and are used for a variety of offences.

### Electronic tagging and curfews

These are intended to enable the police to monitor the whereabouts of offenders and restrict their movements.

### ASBOs

These prevent people from being in an area where they have caused problems for the community in the past.

# Aims of punishment

Magistrates and judges give sentences that are intended to achieve particular aims. You need to know about six aims of punishment (though there are more). Increasingly the authorities are interested in restorative justice.

A recently released prisoner trying on clothes donated by a church

TopFoto

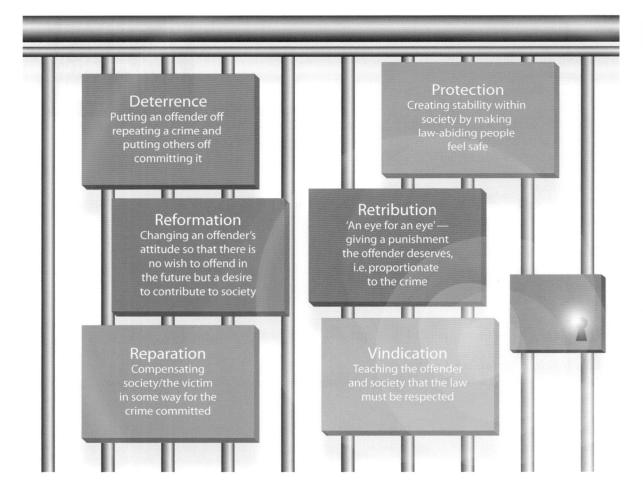

**Deterrence**
Putting an offender off repeating a crime and putting others off committing it

**Protection**
Creating stability within society by making law-abiding people feel safe

**Reformation**
Changing an offender's attitude so that there is no wish to offend in the future but a desire to contribute to society

**Retribution**
'An eye for an eye' — giving a punishment the offender deserves, i.e. proportionate to the crime

**Reparation**
Compensating society/the victim in some way for the crime committed

**Vindication**
Teaching the offender and society that the law must be respected

# Religious views on crime and punishment

 **Buddhism**

| The law | Punishment of offenders | Death penalty (capital punishment) |
|---|---|---|
| ■ Enables practice of dhamma (truth taught by the Buddha)<br>■ To keep law with right intention<br>■ **Engaged Buddhism** might entail civil disobedience/non-violent resistance to authorities — selfless motive | ■ Skilful means to achieve reform/improve kamma — e.g. **Angilumala** organisation<br>■ Example of **Milarepa** (a murderer who changed his ways)<br>■ Protection of society valid aim — First Precept<br>■ Acts as deterrent but is vengeful (Dalai Lama)<br>■ Retribution is against Buddhist thinking — easily becomes revenge and embitters | ■ Most oppose it — against metta, karuna, not use of skilful means<br>■ No chance of reform and improving kamma<br>■ Used by some Buddhist countries for serious offences |

 **Christianity**

| The law | Punishment of offenders |
|---|---|
| ■ Humans have inbuilt moral sense (conscience)<br>■ Original sin leads to crime, along with other factors<br>■ Rulers given authority by God — Romans 13:1–7<br>■ Law to be obeyed unless against God's law — Mark 12:17<br>■ Resistance to law where wrong, e.g. **Desmond Tutu** | ■ Reform central — Jesus always gave second chance<br>■ Unconditional forgiveness — Jesus on the cross, parable of unmerciful servant<br>■ Reparation and vindication important — offenders need to know what they have done<br>■ Protection of society important<br>■ Retribution can become revenge — eye for an eye replaced by Jesus with love of enemy<br>■ Deterrent can be weapon of fear and exploitation<br>■ Many work with offenders and ex-offenders |

## Reformation

| Restorative justice: offenders make amends to their victims (e.g. repairing damage) or meet their victims to talk things through | Education: offenders learn literacy skills, take exams, train in vocational skills |
|---|---|
| Gives offenders a second chance and victims and society a chance to forgive and move on | Those in prison contribute positively to society instead of feeling cut off from it |

| Jesus said: 'Love your enemies and pray for those who persecute you' | 'Forgive us our sins, as we forgive those who have sinned against us' | Example: learning Braille and transcribing books for blind people | Example: the Dartmoor Storybook Dads project helps fathers and their children |
|---|---|---|---|

### Christian views for and against the death penalty

| For the death penalty | Against the death penalty |
|---|---|
| Justice — 'an eye for an eye' — a murderer forfeits his/her own life | The 'eye for an eye' mentality encourages revenge, which is a negative and harmful attitude. Jesus asked God to forgive those who had nailed him to the cross |
| It shows love for the victims of serious crime | It does not show love for one's neighbour or for enemies |
| A second chance is not deserved — the victim doesn't have one | The offender has no chance to reform, to make a fresh start and become a useful citizen |
| The woman in the column opposite had committed adultery, not murder — maybe Jesus' verdict on a murderer would have been different | When Jesus was asked to pass sentence on a woman caught in the act of adultery (a capital offence in first-century Israel), he said those without sin should cast the first stone. He told her that he did not condemn her; she should go but not repeat her sin. He gave her a second chance |
| It provides absolute protection for society | Many murderers are not a danger to society as a whole and, if they are released, it is on licence |
| It is the most effective deterrent | Evidence from the USA shows that the death penalty does not work as a deterrent |
| Forensic science makes execution of innocent people more unlikely | Innocent people have been executed |
| The families of the victim never recover from their trauma — and they are innocent too | It causes deep emotional and psychological trauma to the families of those executed — and they are innocent |

# Hinduism

| The law | Punishment of offenders | Death penalty (capital punishment) |
|---|---|---|
| ▪ Protects society<br>▪ Enables fulfilment of dharma<br>▪ Protest acceptable where government unjust<br>▪ Gandhi's campaign — **satyagraha** (force of truth) | ▪ Essential to deal with negative karma<br>▪ Three elements: retribution, restraint, reformation<br>▪ Status of victim and seriousness of crime taken into account<br>▪ Corporal punishment allowed (but not for Brahmins) | ▪ Used for murder and treason<br>▪ Depends on status of offender and victim — not **Brahmins**<br>▪ Many support it — protection, retribution, deterrence. Deals with bad karma caused by act<br>▪ **Gandhi** against it — goes against principle of ahimsa |

# Islam

| The law | Punishment of offenders | Death penalty (capital punishment) |
|---|---|---|
| ▪ UK Muslims to obey law and respect Shari'ah<br>▪ Protest allowed if law contrary to Islam<br>▪ Force allowed if Islam seriously threatened | ▪ Intended to ensure well-being of society — vindication, protection and deterrence are important aims<br>▪ Retribution central — offender can only be shown mercy when victim receives justice<br>▪ Equality of all in sight of Allah<br>▪ Ideal is honour tempered with mercy<br>▪ Public humiliation accepted in Islamic countries as deterrent and form of justice<br>▪ Prisoners to be treated justly | ▪ For murder and open attack on Islam (Shari'ah law)<br>▪ Life for life approach in Qur'an, accepted by Muhammad<br>▪ Murderers forfeit right to respect for sanctity of life<br>▪ Retribution with honour essential to justice<br>▪ Execution often public — justice and deterrence<br>▪ **Blood money** alternative — financial compensation for next of kin and murderer given life sentence — seen as an act of mercy that will be rewarded by Allah |

 **Judaism**

| The law | Punishment of offenders | Death penalty (capital punishment) |
|---|---|---|
| <ul><li>To obey law of land unless it conflicts with Judaism</li><li>**Beth din** (rabbanic court) deals with religious matters but no legal status — 613 mitzvot</li></ul> | <ul><li>Working out of justice</li><li>Importance of justice, fairness and reparation — this, not retribution, the meaning of an eye for an eye</li><li>Deterrence and protection are important to ensure well-being of society</li><li>Support given to offenders and ex-offenders</li></ul> | <ul><li>Allowed for by Torah as deterrent</li><li>Rarely carried out in Israel — doesn't allow for repentance and change</li><li>Conditions for it almost impossible to fulfil</li><li>Eichmann only person executed in past century — some were against that</li></ul> |

 **Sikhism**

| The law | Punishment of offenders | Death penalty (capital punishment) |
|---|---|---|
| <ul><li>Important to protect vulnerable members of society</li><li>To be obeyed unless it conflicts with Sikh principles — then protest and (as last resort) force permitted</li></ul> | <ul><li>Important to put right what was done wrong to create good karma and achieve justice</li><li>Imprisonment accepted — protection and reform</li><li>Forgiveness encouraged rather than revenge — to respond to evil positively rather than by retaliating</li></ul> | <ul><li>Some accept it — deterrence and protection of society</li><li>Murderers have forfeited right to life — but execution to be humane and not out of desire for revenge</li><li>Many against it — life is sacred</li><li>Prevents chance of repentance and reform — forgiveness, reform and restorative justice preferable</li><li>Risk of wrongful execution</li></ul> |

 **Case study**

# Sister Helen Prejean, CSV

- Born in Louisiana in 1939 and became a nun in 1957
- Became involved in prison work in 1981
- Became the pen pal of a man on Death Row in Louisiana
- Visited him, became his spiritual advisor and was with him as he went to the electric chair

- Seeing what life was like on Death Row and witnessing his death led to her becoming a prominent campaigner against the death penalty
- She also founded 'Survive', an organisation that provides counselling for the families of victims of violence

Reuters
Sister Helen Prejean

- She sees two rights as absolutely fundamental: the right not to be tortured and the right not to be killed
- She believes in the teaching of Jesus not to reply to hate with hate

**Key words**

Angilumala
ASBO
Beth din
blood money
Brahmins
community service
death penalty
Desmond Tutu
deterrence
electronic tagging
engaged Buddhism
fines
Gandhi
Milarepa
parole
prison
probation
protection
reformation
reparation
retribution
satyagraha
vindication

## *Test yourself*

1 Explain briefly why people might commit crime.
2 Name one country that still carries out the death penalty.
3 Name one country that does not carry out the death penalty.
4 In the table below match up correctly each aim of punishment with its explanation.

| Aim of punishment | Explanation of term |
|---|---|
| Deterrence | To compensate society/the victim in some way |
| Protection | To put the offender off committing crime again |
| Reformation | To give the offender what he/she deserves |
| Reparation | To show that the law must be respected |
| Retribution | To keep society safe |
| Vindication | To change the attitude of the offender |

## *Examination question*

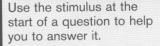
**BREAKING NEWS!** Inspector of prisons slams three prisons over appalling conditions for prisoners!

**a Outline the concerns that many people have about some prisons in the UK.** *(4 marks)*

**Exam tip**

Use the stimulus at the start of a question to help you to answer it.

**b 'Convicted murderers should always receive the death penalty.'**

**Do you agree? Give reasons for your answer, showing that you have thought about more than one point of view. Refer to religious arguments in your answer.**

*(6 marks)*

# Religious attitudes to rich and poor in British society

## Causes and sources of wealth and poverty

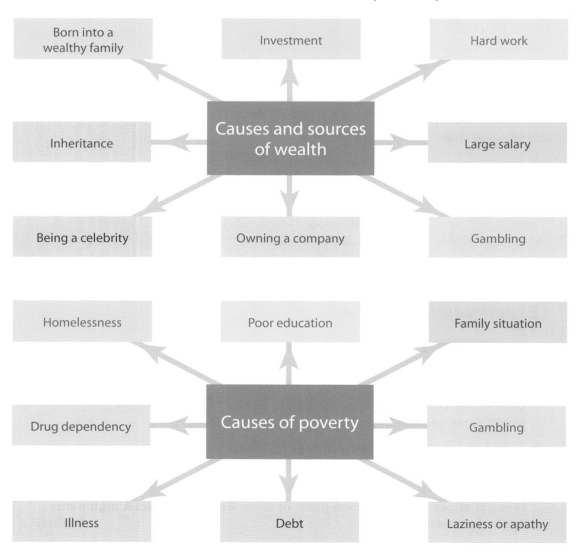

# Breaking free from poverty

There are several ways of breaking free from poverty:

- retraining schemes for the unemployed
- literacy schemes for those with a poor level of education
- ensuring the payment of the **minimum wage**
- benefits and pensions
- advice centres and provision of **counselling**
- provision of affordable housing for rent

# Responsibility for the poor

It is hotly debated where responsibility lies. The following are those generally involved:

- the family
- the local community
- the government
- charities

**Raise money for charity**

**Give enjoyment and excitement** ← **Lotteries** → **Encourage greed**

**Encourage gambling addiction**

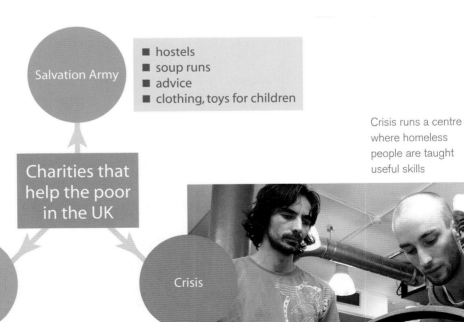

**Salvation Army**

- hostels
- soup runs
- advice
- clothing, toys for children

**Charities that help the poor in the UK**

Crisis runs a centre where homeless people are taught useful skills

**Shelter**

- housing
- advice
- campaigning

**Crisis**

- emergency shelters
- advice
- soup run

Crisis

## Religious attitudes to wealth and poverty

There are additional points on religious attitudes to wealth and poverty in Topic 6, which focuses on world poverty.

 **Buddhism**

- Right livelihood means that making money should not determine one's employment
- Businesses to be run on principles of metta and karuna
- Nothing wrong with being rich and successful — what matters is how the money is acquired and how it is used
- Gambling breaches the First and Fifth Precepts
- Gambling is motivated by greed, so affects kamma

 **Christianity**

- Jesus told the rich man to sell all he had to follow him but the man could not do this
- Jesus praised a rich tax-collector who decided to give half his possessions to charity and compensate generously anyone he had cheated
- According to the New Testament, the love of money (not money in itself) is the root of all evil
- Nothing intrinsically wrong in being rich; it is how people use wealth and their attitude to possessions that matter
- Being rich should be seen as an opportunity to be generous rather than a cause for pride
- Christian employers should create good conditions of employment, pay fair wages and not make profits by unjust means
- Attitudes to **lotteries** vary — some accept them if money raised goes to charity, but others think that they just encourage greed and can lead to gambling addiction
- The Salvation Army and the Church Army (an Anglican organisation) provide hostels and drop-in centres for the homeless, soup runs, advice etc.

Salvation Army volunteers feeding poor children in Chile

# ॐ Hinduism

- Not wrong to be wealthy — it may be the result of good karma in a previous life, and poverty might be the result of wrongdoing in past lives
- **Artha** (acquiring wealth honestly) is one of the four aims in life
- Wealth something to be shared rather than hoarded — many families in India give food to one poor person before each midday meal and give beggars money
- Renunciation of wealth by sadhus is a sign that material possessions are not the most important thing in life
- At **Divali** (festival) business people ask **Lakshmi** (goddess) for success
- Important to treat employees with respect
- Generally opposed to gambling because it encourages greed and the winnings are not gained by honest hard work; it also causes harm (breaching ahimsa) and creates bad karma

Sadhus outside a Hindu temple

# ★ Islam

- Helping the poor is an expression of justice
- Wealth is a blessing from Allah, to be used wisely for others as well as oneself
- **Zakat** is one of the Five Pillars — a tax on income (2.5%) and possessions (e.g. jewellery, property); some of this goes to the poor
- **Sadaqah** is a form of voluntary giving that includes giving money to the poor; should be given secretly as service to Allah
- Employers should ensure good conditions and pay for employees and give them a room for **salah** (prayer)
- Totally opposed to lotteries as gambling is haram

# Judaism

- Wealth is a blessing from God but must be used properly
- **Tzedakah** — the duty to give a tenth of income to be used for the poor
- The best form of tzedakah is that which is given secretly and enables the recipient to become self-reliant — Jewish organisations involved in support of the poor and homeless aim to enable the poor to help themselves and regain their sense of self-worth
- Children have **pushkes** (money boxes) for regular giving from their pocket money — a way of teaching the importance of generosity
- Employers should treat employees fairly — good working conditions and fair wages
- Opposition to lotteries as they are a form of gambling — they encourage greed and might lead to poverty

# Sikhism

- Wealth in itself is not wrong — it is a reward for the previous life
- Poverty is not essential to goodness
- The attitude to wealth is all-important
- Sikhs should share what they own
- Importance of honest work
- Employers to give employees good working conditions and fair wages

| Key words |
|---|
| artha |
| counselling |
| Divali |
| gambling |
| Lakshmi |
| lotteries |
| minimum wage |
| pushkes |
| sadaqah |
| salah |
| tzedakah |
| zakat |

## *Test yourself*

 **Case study**

## Jane

- She constantly argued with her parents as a teenager and one day walked out
- She made her way to London but could not find a job
- She was homeless and was living rough but never turned to drugs
- She was often very hungry and longed for shelter
- The Salvation Army offered her food when they came out on a soup run
- She was offered a place in a Salvation Army hostel and was given advice
- This enabled her to begin to get her life back together
- She was able to get a job and a flat of her own

1 Give three reasons why some people in the UK become poor.
2 Explain how the Salvation Army helped Jane.
3 Explain three ways in which the government helps those who are poor.

## Examination question

**a Outline reasons why many religious believers are against taking part in lotteries.**

*(3 marks)*

### Exam tip

The command word 'outline' indicates that the key features are required and not a detailed description or explanation.

**b 'Religious believers should not be rich.'**

**What do you think? Explain your opinion.**

*(3 marks)*

## Topic 6
# Religious attitudes to world poverty

## The problem of poverty

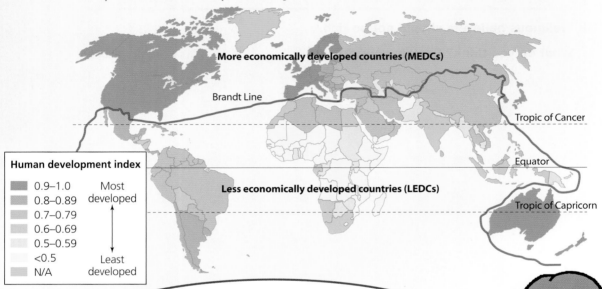

More economically developed countries (MEDCs)

Brandt Line

Tropic of Cancer

Equator

Human development index

- 0.9–1.0
- 0.8–0.89
- 0.7–0.79
- 0.6–0.69
- 0.5–0.59
- <0.5
- N/A

Most developed

↕

Least developed

Less economically developed countries (LEDCs)

Tropic of Capricorn

Hi! I'm Liz. I'm 13 and I live in the UK.
I go to the local comp, which is only a mile down the road,
but my mum takes me in the car every day, so I don't have to get up early.
I love weekends, as then I go down to town with my friends —
we sometimes buy DVDs or clothes if our mums are feeling generous,
and we always go for a burger. I hope to go to uni and
then work in a big law firm.

Hi! I'm Grace. I'm 13 and I live in Uganda.
My parents both died of AIDS when I was little and I hardly
remember them. Luckily, my aunt said she would look after me even though
she's a widow, so I live with her and my three young cousins. But we don't
have enough money for me to go to school so I help her with the animals.
I also fetch water and sometimes prepare the meal that we have once
a day. I'd love to become a teacher, but that's just a dream
— I can't read or write.

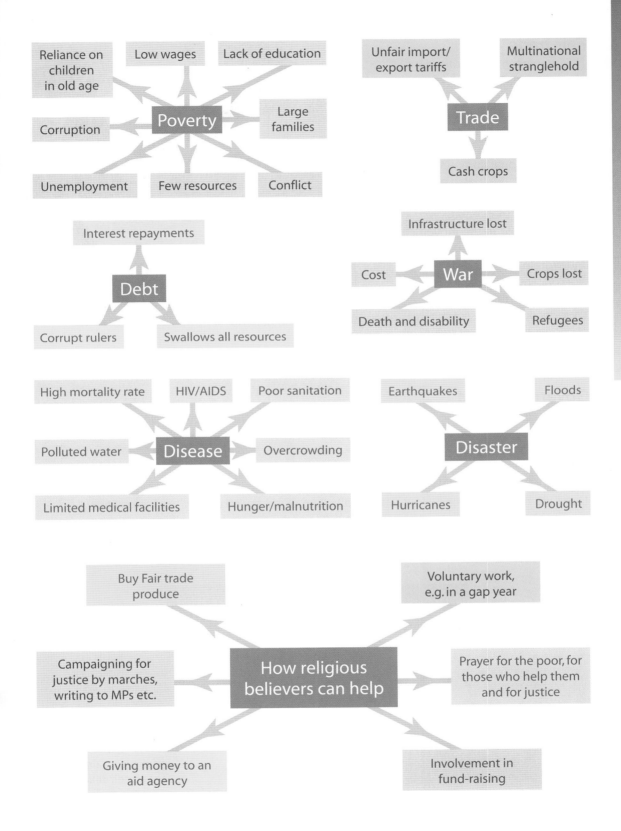

Poverty

Reliance on children in old age

Low wages

Lack of education

Corruption

Large families

Unemployment

Few resources

Conflict

Trade

Unfair import/export tariffs

Multinational stranglehold

Cash crops

Debt

Interest repayments

Corrupt rulers

Swallows all resources

War

Infrastructure lost

Cost

Crops lost

Death and disability

Refugees

Disease

High mortality rate

HIV/AIDS

Poor sanitation

Polluted water

Overcrowding

Limited medical facilities

Hunger/malnutrition

Disaster

Earthquakes

Floods

Hurricanes

Drought

How religious believers can help

Buy Fair trade produce

Voluntary work, e.g. in a gap year

Campaigning for justice by marches, writing to MPs etc.

Prayer for the poor, for those who help them and for justice

Giving money to an aid agency

Involvement in fund-raising

# Fair trade

This movement was started by a number of aid agencies and organisations. **Fair trade** aims to remove the injustice at the heart of much world trade, e.g. those who work on banana plantations for multinational companies are very poorly paid. It also aims to give the producers of goods a fair wage for their goods.

Those involved in the movement also aim to provide decent living and working conditions for the workers, including schools for children and medical care.

They encourage the setting up of cooperatives and of using suitable technology. They promote **sustainable development**.

Fair trade is about better prices, decent working conditions, local sustainability and fair terms of trade for farmers and workers in the developing world

## Government aid

A small percentage of the UK's national income is given annually to projects in LEDCs to help reduce poverty. In an emergency, e.g. the 2004 Asian tsunami, large sums are given for immediate relief.

## Aid given by charities

There are many aid agencies working to alleviate world poverty. They are increasingly involved in campaigning to change the attitudes of those who have political and economic power, as well as in long-term projects. In a crisis they work together to deal with the emergency more effectively.

Types of aid given to poor countries

Emergency aid

Aid given in the short term to help people survive in a crisis

Long-term aid

Aid given over a few years to fund projects aimed at enabling self-reliance

CAFOD activists lobbying parliament to make poverty history

## Religious views on world poverty

All religious believers want to see an end to world poverty. Their views are based on three key ideas:

- **Justice:** each person has the right to fair and equal treatment.
- **Stewardship:** humans are responsible for looking after those in need.
- **Compassion:** literally 'suffering with', this means feeling pity for others and wanting to do something to help.

There are additional points on religious attitudes to wealth and poverty in Topic 5, which focuses on wealth and poverty in British society.

 **Buddhism**

- Selfish craving is the direct cause of suffering
- Greed is one of the six poisons and generosity one of the six perfections
- To reach nibbana, humans have to practise the magga, avoiding extremes of poverty and wealth
- Right viewpoint, right intention and right action are fulfilled through selfless caring for others
- Dana is a central feature of Buddhism, expressing metta and karuna

### The Karuna Trust

- Works with the most disadvantaged in India, especially **Dalits**
- Aims to give people a sense of dignity and move them out of poverty
- Runs schools and hostels for children whose parents cannot afford to keep them if they are not working
- Trains local women as health workers
- Runs an AIDS project
- Supports cultural activities

- Love of God and neighbour the two greatest commandments, according to Jesus
- Rich people cannot claim to love God if they ignore the needs of the poor (1 John 3:17)
- Jesus' parable of the sheep and goats teaches that whatever humans do or fail to do, they do or fail to do for him
- His parable of the Good Samaritan teaches that one's neighbour is everyone, regardless of race or culture
- His parable of the rich man and Lazarus is a warning that Christians have no excuse for not helping the poor

## Christian Aid

- Started as agency to help refugees in Europe at end of the Second World War
- Committed to seeing a just world now, not just in the future — one of its slogans
- Belief in life before death — one of its slogans
- Works on development projects with partner organisations in countries all over the world
- Involved in both emergency and long-term aid
- Also works with other UK agencies
- Founder member of Fair trade movement
- Involved in many campaigns to get rid of debt, unfair trade, war etc.
- Annual Christian Aid week — envelopes put through as many UK letterboxes as possible and then collected by volunteers

- Wealth to be shared rather than hoarded
- One of five daily duties is to give to the poor
- Many British Hindus give to projects involved with the poor in India
- Generous giving builds up good karma

## Sewa International

- Responds to disasters whatever their cause, e.g. appealed for money to help with drought in Kenya
- Works through partner organisations

# ☪ Islam

- Zakat is one of Five Pillars — some of it given to the poor
- Ramadan fast helps Muslims empathise with the poor and become more compassionate
- **Zakat-ul-Fitr** is an extra donation, usually cost of a meal for each family member
- At end of **Id-ul-Adha** (festival), pilgrims sacrifice animal; its meat tinned and exported for poor and is known as **qurbani meat**. Those not on **hajj** (pilgrimage to Makkah) often give money instead
- Cannot be a Muslim and let someone go hungry (Hadith)

## Muslim Aid

- Works through partner organisations
- Responds to emergencies and often works in conjunction with other charities
- Many long-term projects
- Involved in the Make Poverty History campaign

#  Judaism

- Generosity is a key part of the Torah
- Instructions to defend the orphan and widow, i.e. the most vulnerable members of society
- Justice matters more than ritual (Amos)

## Tzedek

- Works worldwide regardless of religion etc.
- Sends volunteers to work alongside local people, concentrating on small, local self-help projects
- Many long-term projects
- Educates Jewish communities and schools about global poverty

#  Sikhism

- Equality of all means that all should have equal access to life's necessities
- Importance of compassion, e.g. Bhai Ghaniya giving water to the wounded of both sides in battle
- Cannot love God if one fails to love other human beings

## Khalsa Aid

- Set up by UK Sikhs in 1999 to help victims of war in Kosovo
- Concerned with emergency aid
- Helps anyone in need, whatever their race, culture or religion

## Test yourself

1 Give four facts about a religious aid organisation that you have studied in the chart below.

Religious organisation that works to alleviate world povery

2 Explain the difference between emergency and long-term aid.

## Examination question

Do you like my new skirt and top? I went to that big store on the high street and I was really lucky. My mum gave me some money to treat myself, and because they were so cheap, I had enough to go and buy some earrings that I've been wanting for ages. I really couldn't believe how cheap they were — I got a real bargain. And they were made in India — so I feel as if I've been helping the poor.

You must be joking. That store was on the news last week — an undercover reporter had discovered that those who make clothes for it are really exploited — they work long hours in awful conditions for almost nothing. If you really want to help the poor, be more careful where you shop.

**a** Explain how the Fair trade movement seeks to help workers in poor nations. *(3 marks)*

**b** 'If people have poor working conditions, their own governments should sort it out. It's not our concern.'

Do you agree? Give reasons for your answer, showing that you have thought about more than one point of view. Refer to religious arguments in your answer. *(6 marks)*

### Exam tip

You are expected to know about the work of religious organisations that are concerned with relieving global poverty. Make sure that the organisation you research is a religious one.

# Key word index